A Midsummer Night's Dream

Contents

What's it all about?	3
Who's who?	4
Midsummer Day	6
Lovers and madmen	7
Dream-time	9
Robin Goodfellow	10
Naughty, naughty	11
You ladies	12
That's entertainment!	13
A play within a play	15
What do you think?	16

OXFORD
UNIVERSITY PRESS

Great Clarendon Street, Oxford OX2 6DP

Oxford University Press is a department of the University of Oxford.
It furthers the University's objective of excellence in research,
scholarship, and education by publishing worldwide in

Oxford New York

Auckland Cape Town Dar es Salaam Hong Kong Karachi
Kuala Lumpur Madrid Melbourne Mexico City Nairobi
New Delhi Shanghai Taipei Toronto

With offices in

Argentina Austria Brazil Chile Czech Republic France Greece
Guatemala Hungary Italy Japan South Korea Poland Portugal
Singapore Switzerland Thailand Turkey Ukraine Vietnam

Oxford is a registered trade mark of Oxford University Press in the UK
and in certain other countries

Text © Alison Smith 2009

The moral rights of the author have been asserted

Database right Oxford University Press (maker)

First published 2009

All rights reserved. No part of this publication may be reproduced,
stored in a retrieval system, or transmitted in any form or by any
means, without the prior permission in writing of Oxford University
Press, or as expressly permitted by law, or under terms agreed with the
appropriate reprographics rights organization. Enquiries concerning
reproduction outside the scope of the above should be sent to the
Rights Department, Oxford University Press, at the address above.

You must not circulate this book in any other binding or cover and you
must impose this same condition on any acquirer.

British Library Cataloguing in Publication Data

Data available

ISBN 978 019 8329343

10 9 8 7 6 5 4 3 2 1

Printed in Great Britain by Bell and Bain Ltd., Glasgow

Mixed Sources
Product group from well-managed
forests and other controlled sources
www.fsc.org Cert no. TT-COC-002769
© 1996 Forest Stewardship Council

FSC

Acknowledgements

The publisher would like to thank the following for permission to
reproduce photographs: p.9 © Photostage; p.10 Robin Goodfellow,
from 'A Midsummer Nights Dream II.1'. By William Shakespeare
(1564 – 1616) (woodcut) (b/w photo), © English School,
(16th century)/Private Collection/The Bridgeman Art Library;
p.15 © Robbie Jack/Corbis; p.16 © Fox Searchlight Pictures

Design and illustrations by Steve Evans

Cover illustration by Silke Bachmann

What's it all about?

Dreams

The role of women

Love

A Midsummer Night's Dream is one of Shakespeare's best known comedy plays, and as a comedy it has to have a happy ending. It is made-up of four, quite separate stories that run alongside one another, and sometimes combine. These are:

- Theseus and Hippolyta celebrating their wedding
- the group of young lovers who run away into the wood
- the mechanicals rehearsing their play
- Oberon and Titania quarrelling over a changeling boy.

Magic

The criss-crossing of storylines is partly what makes the play so funny. Bottom stumbles out of his rehearsal and into Oberon's feud with Titania. Puck meddles with the destinies of the young lovers and Hippolyta comments that the play is 'the silliest stuff' that she ever heard. How else do the stories intertwine?

Rivalry

> **What's so funny?**
> Talk to your partner about what makes something funny. Is it just someone telling jokes? Or is it something else? Explain your ideas clearly.

There are some **themes** that run through the play as a whole. Have a look at the themes scattered around this page. Which do you think are most important and why?

Friendship

Metatheatre
Where characters make the audience aware that they are watching a play: maybe a character will notice the audience and speak to it, or characters will actually put on a play of their own!

Marriage

Metatheatre

Festivities

A Midsummer Night's Dream

Who's who?

The key characters

The Athenian Court

Theseus
- Duke of Athens
- engaged to Hippolyta

Hippolyta
- Queen of the Amazons
- engaged to Theseus

Egeus
- a member of the Athenian Court
- Hermia's father

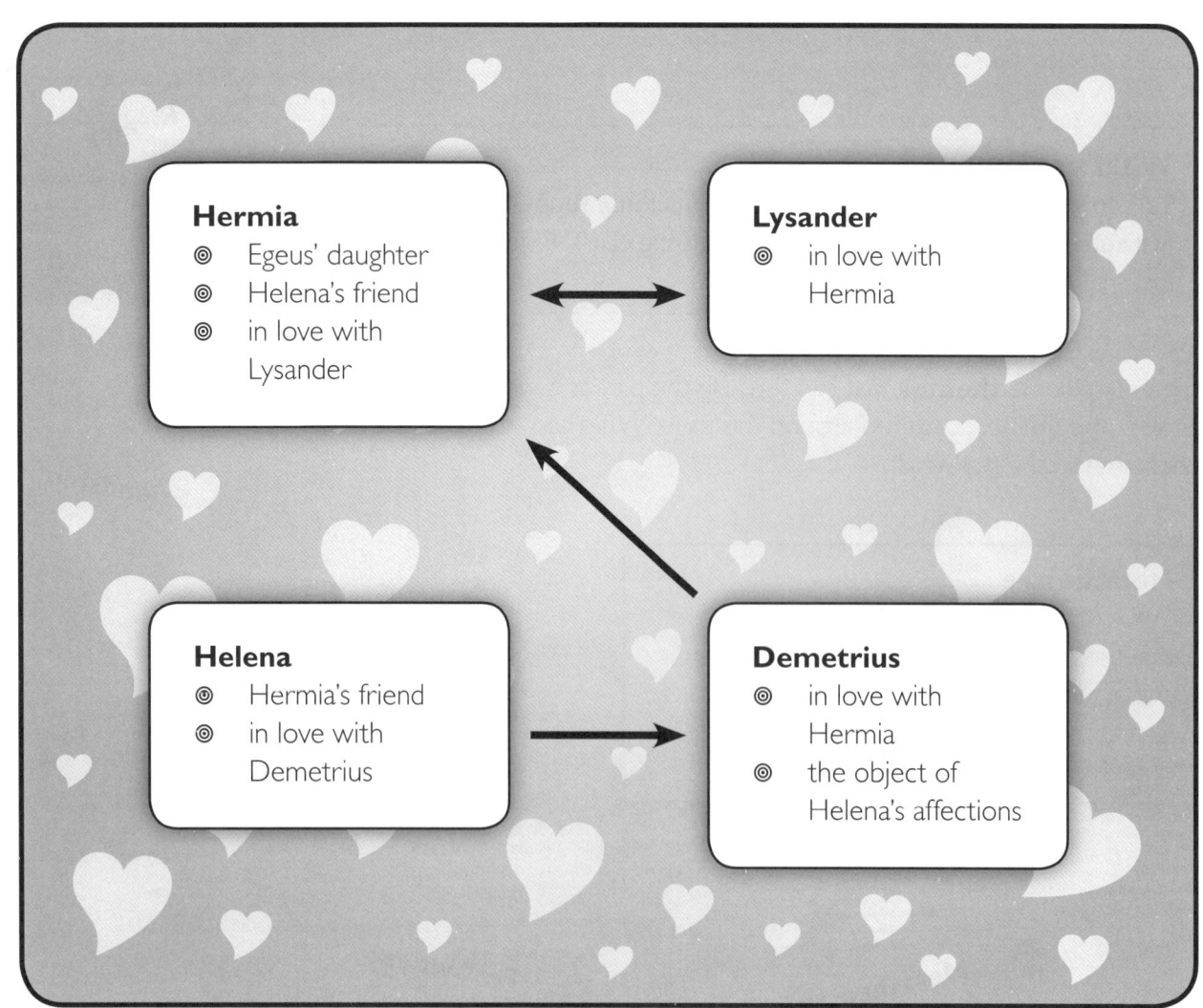

Hermia
- Egeus' daughter
- Helena's friend
- in love with Lysander

Lysander
- in love with Hermia

Helena
- Hermia's friend
- in love with Demetrius

Demetrius
- in love with Hermia
- the object of Helena's affections

A Midsummer Night's Dream

Who's who?

The fairies

Oberon
- King of the fairies
- in a feud with Titania at the start of the play

Titania
- Fairy Queen
- in a feud with Oberon at the start of the play

Puck
- also known as Robin Goodfellow
- a fairy servant to Oberon
- playful and mischievous

The mechanicals

Peter Quince
- a carpenter
- director of the play, put on at Theseus' wedding

Snug
- a joiner
- plays the lion

Nick Bottom
- a weaver
- plays Pyramus but wants to play all the parts

Francis Flute
- a bellows-mender
- plays Thisbe

Tom Snout
- a tinker
- plays 'Wall'

Robin Starveling
- a tailor
- plays 'Moonshine'

A Midsummer Night's Dream

Midsummer Day

People in Shakespeare's day would have known exactly what to expect from the title of the play. Perhaps to a modern audience, things are not as clear.

Midsummer Day is the 24th of June, and people believed that it was one of the most magical days of the year. Some of the things they believed were:

- that spirits were at their most powerful on midsummer night
- that flowers gathered on this night could be used to perform magic
- that your dreams on midsummer night might reveal your true love
- that you might go insane!

Discuss it!
Think about the play as a whole. How many examples of midsummer beliefs can you find?

Fairy toys

What else can you find out about the beliefs of the day? What did Elizabethans think about magic and fairies? You could start by researching in the library and on the Internet.

When you've collected information on the topic, make a fact sheet to inform other people. You could copy the template on the right or design your own. Think about how you might illustrate it to make it more informative.

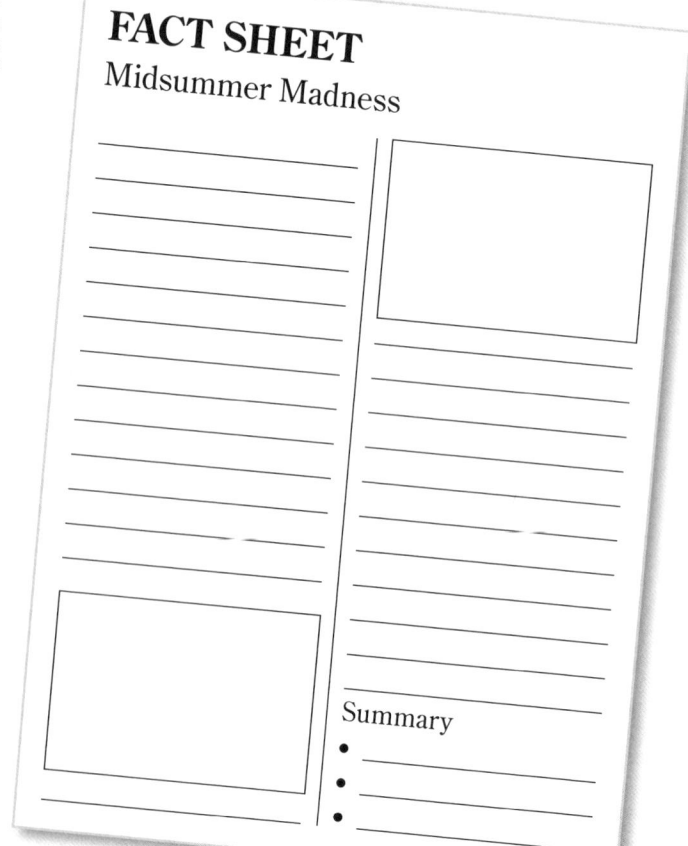

FACT SHEET
Midsummer Madness

Summary

Lovers and madmen

In this play, different people have different ideas about love. Look at the characters below and try to match them with their views:

Egeus

Lysander

Theseus

Demetrius

Helena

Oberon

Hermia

Puck

1 – Is in love, but it is **unrequited**. Also, someone loves him, but he doesn't love her back.

2 – Believes that love can make people crazy but also that marriage makes life enjoyable.

3 – Tells his girlfriend to run away from her family so they can be together.

4 – Believes that if a daughter loves her father, she will do as she is told.

5 – Is able to manipulate love using magic.

6 – Is in love, but it is **unrequited**.

7 – Is in love, but is also quite tired of someone who loves her.

8 – Uses love as a method to get what he wants.

Activity answers

1 – Demetrius; 2 – Theseus; 3 – Lysander; 4 – Egeus; 5 – Puck; 6 – Helena; 7 – Hermia; 8 – Oberon

A Midsummer Night's Dream

LOVERS AND MADMEN

PROBLEM PAGE

By the end of Act 1, the young Athenians are having lots of problems with their relationships. Imagine that you are either Helena or Hermia; Lysander or Demetrius. Write a letter to the problem page of a magazine. Explain what has happened to you and how it makes you feel. Make sure that you base it on what has happened in the play so far.

Unrequited love – love that is not returned.

You might begin with something like:

> Dear Auntie Mildred,
>
> I just don't know what to do. I am so in love with a boy. He's absolutely gorgeous, but the thing is – he's in love with my best friend...

MAKE-UP AND BREAK-UP

Over the course of the play, all the relationships seem to take twists and turns, proving that love is rarely an easy journey.

Choose three of the characters from the play and make a flow chart showing how their relationships change as time goes on. Use the symbols below and connect them with a flow-line. If you can, try to pick out a quote from the play to go with each item on the chart. The example on the right shows how this might look for Theseus. His relationship is quite straightforward; this is not the case for some of the characters!

- ☐ **The start or end of something**
- ◇ **A decision**
- ☐ **A development in the relationship**
- ⊃ **A delay**
- ▱ **Input or output of information**
- → **Flow-line**

Theseus meets Hippolyta at war, before the play starts.
I...won thy love doing thee injuries

↓

Theseus plans to marry Hippolyta.
I will wed thee in another key

↓

Time passes slowly before the wedding. *how slow/This old moon wanes!*

←

The wedding celebrations begin. *What revels are in hand?*

A MIDSUMMER NIGHT'S DREAM

Dream-time

One of the key themes of the play is the difference between dreams and reality. Dreams often warn characters of things that are about to happen, or they are used to solve problems.

> **What does it mean?**
> Think about the things that you often dream about. Some people think that dreams tell you about your life; do you agree?

At the end of the play Puck tells the audience that if they didn't like the play, then they should think of it as a dream that they can wake up from:

If we shadows have offended,
Think but this, and all is mended:
That you have but slumber'd here
While these visions did appear;

What other similarities are there between the play and dreams?

Imagine...

...that you are going to write your own comedy based on a dream. You need to think about:

- what characters might be in the dream
- where the dream will be set
- the things that will happen in the dream
- how you will present it. For example: a play, film or cartoon.

When you have planned the comedy, you will present the idea to the class, who will choose the best concept.

Photo of a performance of A Midsummer Night's Dream by the Footsbarn Theatre Company, 2008

Then I woke up

Now think again about *A Midsummer Night's Dream*. Why are dreams important to the following characters in the play? What dreams do they have?

Nick Bottom   **Hermia**   **Lysander**   **Helena**
          Titania   **Demetrius**

A Midsummer Night's Dream

Robin Goodfellow

Robin Goodfellow and Hobgoblin are both names for Puck, Oberon's fairy servant in the play. Puck is able to move between the different worlds and has an important impact on everyone he meets.

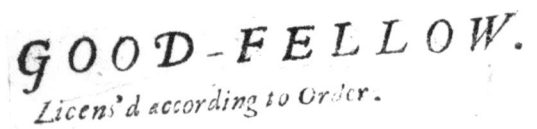

A sixteenth-century woodcut of Robin Goodfellow

Although we know that Shakespeare probably made up the plot of this play, the character Puck was already known to audiences, through myth and legend. Elizabethans would have associated Puck with:

- shape-shifting – becoming different things at will
- helping around the house – only if you were on his good side!
- leading travellers astray – with a mystical light
- playing pranks – such as tripping people up, rolling them out of bed, blowing out candles.

Look at the conversation below, which is the first time that we meet Puck, and see if you can find evidence of any of these things:

Fairy
Are not you he
That frights the maidens of the villagery,
Skim milk, and sometimes labour in the quern,
And bootless make the breathless housewife churn,
And sometime make the drink to bear no barm,
Mislead night-wanderers, laughing at their harm?
Those that 'Hobgoblin' call you, and 'Sweet Puck',
You do their work, and they shall have good luck.
Are not you he?

Puck
Thou speakest aright;
I am that merry wanderer of the night.
I jest to Oberon, and make him smile
When I a fat and bean-fed horse beguile,
Neighing in likeness of a filly foal;
And sometime lurk I in a gossip's bowl
In very likeness of a roasted crab,
And when she drinks, against her lips I bob,
And on her wither'd dewlap pour the ale.
The wisest aunt, telling the saddest tale,
Sometime for threefoot stool mistaketh me;
Then slip I from her bum, down topples she,
And 'Tailor' cries, and falls into a cough;
And then the whole choir hold their hips and loffe,
And waxen in their mirth, and neeze, and swear
A merrier hour was never wasted there.

What mischief!

Look through the rest of the play for evidence of Puck's mischievous behaviour. How important do you think he is to the way the play turns out? Why?

Naughty, Naughty

One thing that helps to create chaos and resulting humour in the play is bad behaviour. Puck is one of the worst-behaved characters, but there are plenty of others who do things they shouldn't.

For each of the following characters, make a list of the unruly things they say and do. Think about why each character behaves like this and what their actions lead to:

- Oberon
- Puck
- Hermia
- Lysander
- Bottom

School report

Imagine that you are a teacher and have to write a report for each of these characters. You have to explain to their parents that their behaviour is unacceptable but without making it sound *too* bad.
You could start:

Report of: PUCK

Date _____

Absences: _____

Puck is a lively and enthusiastic young man who sometimes lets his behaviour get in the way of his learning. I am sure that you would agree that pulling chairs out from under people is not acceptable behaviour.

Grades

Behaviour ☐
Effort ☐
Problem-solving ☐
Team-work ☐

Try to give the character a grade for each of the criteria on the report. Be prepared to justify your choices. You may have to discuss them at parents' evening!

A Midsummer Night's Dream

YOU LADIES

In Shakespeare's England, the role of women in society was very different to what it is today. We get a sense of this at the start of the play, when Egeus says of Hermia:

> As she is mine, I may dispose of her

What do you think of this view? Do you agree with it? Explain why.

Look closely:
What do we find out in Act 1, Scene 1 about how women were thought of in Shakespeare's day?

Then think about what the following characters say about women:

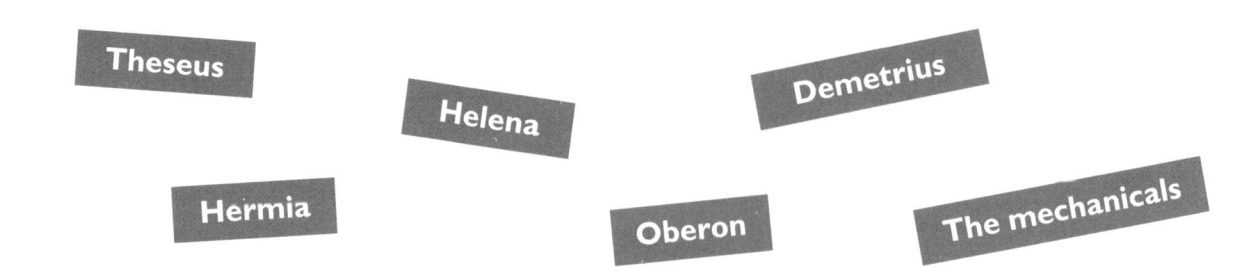

- Theseus
- Helena
- Demetrius
- Hermia
- Oberon
- The mechanicals

Make a fact sheet to inform an Elizabethan woman what is expected of her. You will need to make it detailed enough to be useful.

Talk to your partner. Why do you think people behaved like this? It's not as simple as saying they were just sexist. You might need to do some further research.

A MIDSUMMER NIGHT'S DREAM

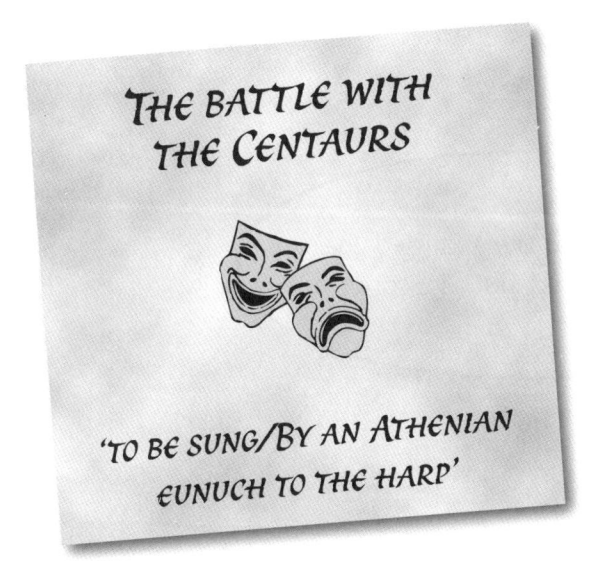

That's entertainment!

These days, at weddings, we are likely to have a meal and a disco, maybe with an entertainer for the kids. In Shakespeare's day, though, it would have been quite normal for wealthy people to have a play performed for their entertainment; even Queen Elizabeth had one.

> **Disco inferno**
> Talk to your partner about what kind of entertainment would be best for a wedding. What kind of mood would you want it to create? Why?

Queen Elizabeth was rich enough to pay for a play to be written especially for her. In *A Midsummer Night's Dream*, Theseus and Hippolyta have a list to choose from. Look at the flyers below and decide which of them you would prefer to watch at a wedding. Explain why.

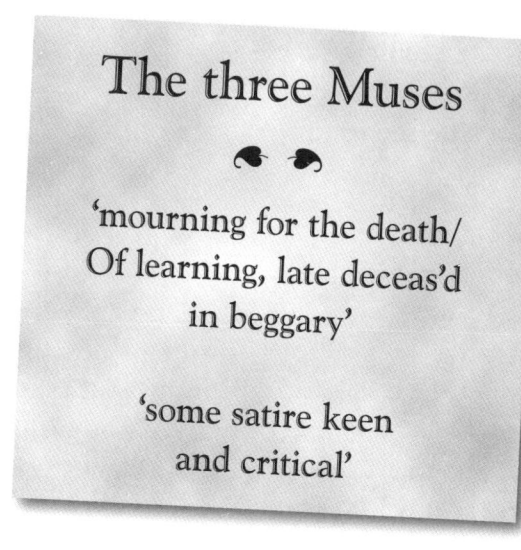

THE BATTLE WITH THE CENTAURS

'TO BE SUNG/BY AN ATHENIAN EUNUCH TO THE HARP'

The riot of the tipsy Bacchanals

'Tearing the Thracian singer in their rage'

'an old device'

The three Muses

'mourning for the death/ Of learning, late deceas'd in beggary'

'some satire keen and critical'

Pyramus and Thisbe

'A tedious brief scene of young Pyramus/ And his love Thisbe, very tragical mirth'

A MIDSUMMER NIGHT'S DREAM

THAT'S ENTERTAINMENT!

The chosen entertainment for the wedding turns out to be the play that Peter Quince and his friends have been rehearsing. Look how Quince introduces it:

> If we offend, it is with our good will.
> That you should think, we come not to offend,
> But with good will. To show our simple skill,
> That is the true beginning of our end.
> Consider then, we come but in despite.
> We do not come as minding to content you,
> Our true intent is. All for your delight,
> We are not here. That you should here repent you,
> The actors are at hand; and by their show
> You shall know all that you are like to know.

In response to this, Theseus comments:

> His speech was like a tangled chain, nothing impaired, but all disordered.

Theseus is right; what Quince says certainly makes sense, but because he's got his punctuation muddled up, he doesn't say what he means. Rather than telling the audience that the play is going to be excellent, he seems to be warning them that it might be a complete disaster.

With a partner, look through the extract above and work out what it seems like Quince is saying, and what he really means. Here is an example to help you:

> If we offend, it is /
> with our good will.

It seems like he is telling them that the point of the play is to offend them. What he meant to say was that if they are offended, he's sorry because that wasn't their intention.

A play within a play

Part of the opening of the play, known as the **prologue**, goes like this:

> **Prologue**
> A speech given before the play starts. This was often used to explain what was going to happen so that people wouldn't get confused.

By moonshine did these lovers think no scorn
To meet at Ninus' tomb, there, there to woo.
This grisly beast, which Lion hight by name,
The trusty Thisbe, coming first by night,
Did scare away, or rather did affright;
And as she fled, her mantle she did fall,
Which Lion vile with bloody mouth did stain.
Anon comes Pyramus, sweet youth and tall,
And finds his trusty Thisbe's mantle slain;
Whereat with blade, with bloody, blameful blade,
He bravely broach'd his boiling bloody breast;
And Thisbe, tarrying in mulberry shade,
His dagger drew, and died. For all the rest,
Let Lion, Moonshine, Wall, and lovers twain
At large discourse, while here they do remain.

Photo of a performance of A Midsummer Night's Dream at The Open Air Theatre, London, 1994

> **On stage**
> In a small group, act out a version of the prologue for the rest of the class.
> You will need to decide what costumes and props you will need.

Round of applause?

Do you think that the play was a successful choice for a wedding?
Discuss with your partner. What was good about it? What was bad about it?

Did the wedding guests think it was a success?

What do you think?

A Midsummer Night's Dream has always been a popular play and even when theatre was banned, people got around the ban by just performing *Pyramus and Thisbe*. However, a man called Samuel Pepys, who saw the play in the 1660s, described it in his diary as:

...the most insipid, ridiculous play that ever I saw

That didn't stop people putting it on, though. In the Victorian period, there was a version which included live rabbits, and one with a cast of over 100 people. Since then, plenty of other versions have been made; including films. Even *High School Musical 2* is loosely based on it.

Describe it

Discuss with the group which of the following adjectives you would use to describe the play. You should be ready to explain why.

Poster for the 1999 film, directed by Michael Hoffman

Terrifying

Hilarious

Fast-paced

Romantic

Poignant

Disturbing

Optimistic

Depressing

Dreamlike

Tense

Enchanting

Slow-paced

Action-packed

Original

Write a review

Now write your own review of the play, saying what its strengths and weaknesses are.

You'll need to think about who the audience is, so that you get the tone right. For example, you'd need to use a different style of writing for teachers than you would for students.

A Midsummer Night's Dream